HOW TO FLY A 747

BY IAN GRAHAM

CANDLEWICK PRESS
CAMBRIDGE, MASSACHUSETTS

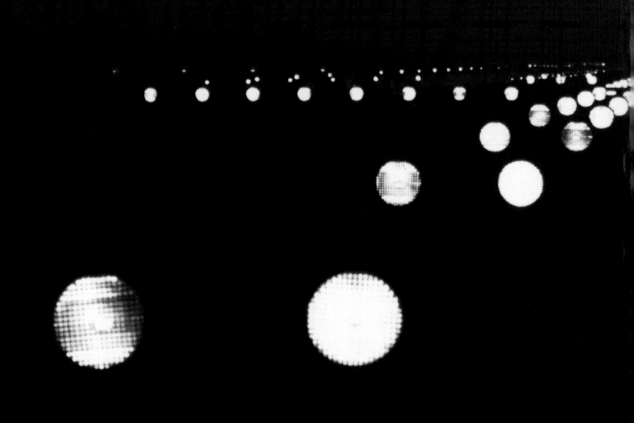

AWN IS BREAKING over the runway as you arrive at the airport. Today is a special day, because soon YOU are going to learn how to fly the world's largest passenger plane—the Boeing 747-400.

The 747-400 is gigantic—as tall as a six-story building and longer than 17 cars. You will take the controls of this massive jet and fly its 436 passengers and crew thousands of miles across the globe. Welcome aboard, Captain!

FLIGHT DECK

This is the flight deck, your plane's command center. Your seat is on the left. The one on the right is for your First Officer, the copilot, who will assist you during the flight. Make yourself comfortable and fasten your seat belt.

FLIGHT CONTROLS

All around you are hundreds of instruments. You will use these to control everything that happens from takeoff to landing.

The biggest instruments are the computer screens that run across the front of your flight deck, below the windshields. These will help you to fly the plane safely. (You will find out more about them on page 16.)

⬆ ALL OF THE CONTROLS are designed to be within easy reach.

THIRD PILOT

The panel below the windshields is your autopilot. This is a computer system that you can program to fly the plane for you. Normally pilots switch on the autopilot as soon as the plane has taken off. You won't be using the autopilot today though, as you're going to learn how to fly.

ARE YOU READY FOR TAKEOFF?

⬆ THE FLIGHT DECK is at the top of the plane, giving the pilots a bird's-eye view.

RADIO MAGNETIC INDICATOR
(see page 15)

COMPUTER SCREENS (see page 16)

AUTOPILOT PANEL (see page 4)

CAPTAIN'S SEAT

FIRST OFFICER'S SEAT

CONTROL COLUMN
(see page 7)

WING FLAPS LEVER (see page 21)

WHEELS LEVER (see page 22)

ENGINE POWER LEVERS (see page 8)

WEATHER RADAR SWITCH (see page 18)

⬆ YOUR FLIGHT DECK

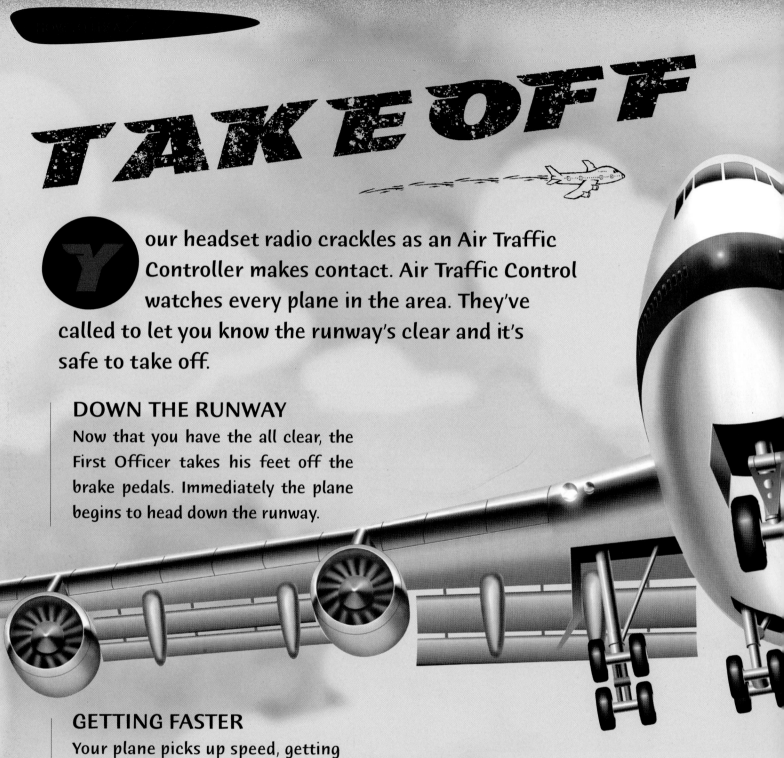

TAKE OFF

Your headset radio crackles as an Air Traffic Controller makes contact. Air Traffic Control watches every plane in the area. They've called to let you know the runway's clear and it's safe to take off.

DOWN THE RUNWAY

Now that you have the all clear, the First Officer takes his feet off the brake pedals. Immediately the plane begins to head down the runway.

GETTING FASTER

Your plane picks up speed, getting faster all the time. Your First Officer calls,

"V1."

This stands for Velocity 1 (velocity means speed).

If something is wrong and you need to abandon the takeoff, you must do it NOW. You're traveling so fast that soon there won't be enough runway left for you to stop.

TAKEOFF

Within seconds you are traveling at hundreds of miles per hour. You are ready to rotate, or lift, your plane's nose into the air. The First Officer calls,

"Rotate."

You pull back the control column a little, the front wheels begin to leave the ground, and you are airborne.

CONTROL COLUMN

⬆ KEEP THE CONTROL COLUMN pulled toward you to climb higher into the air.

"V2,"

calls the First Officer as you reach Velocity 2. This is the speed you need to be traveling to climb higher into the air. You pull right back on the control column and soar upward.

✈ A FULLY LOADED JUMBO JET HURTLES DOWN THE RUNWAY AT ABOUT 195 MILES PER HOUR JUST BEFORE IT TAKES OFF— THAT'S ABOUT THE SAME AS THE TOP SPEED OF A FORMULA 1 RACING CAR!

ENGINES

Hold the control column back to keep on climbing. Your plane is now traveling at over 198 miles per hour. It's powered through the sky by four giant jet engines—each one the size of a family car.

⬆ THE 747 has four engines: two on each wing.

ENGINE FOOD

Like car engines, the 747's jet engines need fuel to make them work. Jet planes use a fuel called kerosene— lots and lots of it! Your plane can carry enough to fill 10 fuel trucks!

The 747-400 has eight fuel tanks—three in each wing, one in the floor of the plane's body and one in the tail.

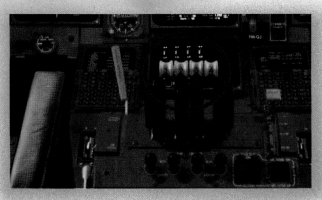

⬆ THE POWER LEVERS are by your right hand.

POWER LEVERS

You have four power levers; one for each engine. Pushing the levers forward sends more fuel to the engines. More fuel makes them work faster and pushes the plane along more quickly. Pulling the levers back slows the plane down.

1 FAN-TASTIC

Like most modern jet planes, your 747-400 is powered by engines called turbofans. At the front of each engine is a giant fan that spins very quickly, sucking in air.

2 COLD AIR

Most of the air is pushed straight around the engine, to rush out of the back at high speed. This cold air produces most of the thrust—the force that pushes the plane forward.

PLANE GOES THIS WAY

⬅ - - - - - - - - - - - -

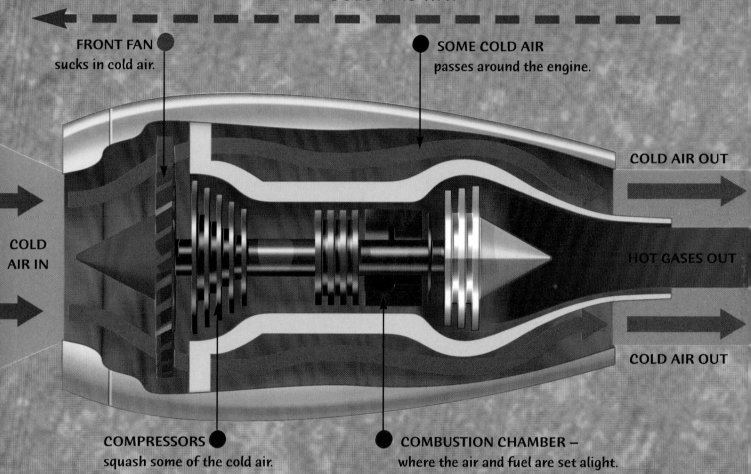

FRONT FAN sucks in cold air.

SOME COLD AIR passes around the engine.

COLD AIR IN

COLD AIR OUT

HOT GASES OUT

COLD AIR OUT

COMPRESSORS squash some of the cold air.

COMBUSTION CHAMBER — where the air and fuel are set alight.

3 SQUASHED AIR

The rest of the air is sucked into smaller fans called compressors. These squash the air and force it into the combustion chamber. Here it is mixed with fuel and set alight.

4 HOT AIR

When the air-fuel mixture is burned, it produces hot gases that shoot out of the back of the engine. These hot gases produce more thrust to help push your plane through the sky.

WINGS

As vitally important as the engines are, you would be lost without the two huge wings stretching out from your plane. You wouldn't get far without those wings—in fact, you wouldn't even get off the runway!

SPECIAL SHAPE

Plane wings are a special shape— curved on top and flat underneath. The curve means that the air flowing over the wing has farther to travel than the air below—and has to go faster to keep up!

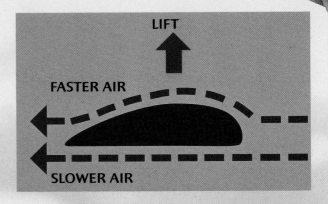

SPOILERS

FLAPS

AILERONS

FLAPS

LIFT

The faster-moving air sucks the wing upward. This sucking force is called lift. You need a lot of it to keep a plane the size of a 747 in the air—that's why your plane has such massive wings!

LIFT

FASTER AIR

SLOWER AIR

⬆ **LIFT IS CREATED** when air flows faster above the wing than below.

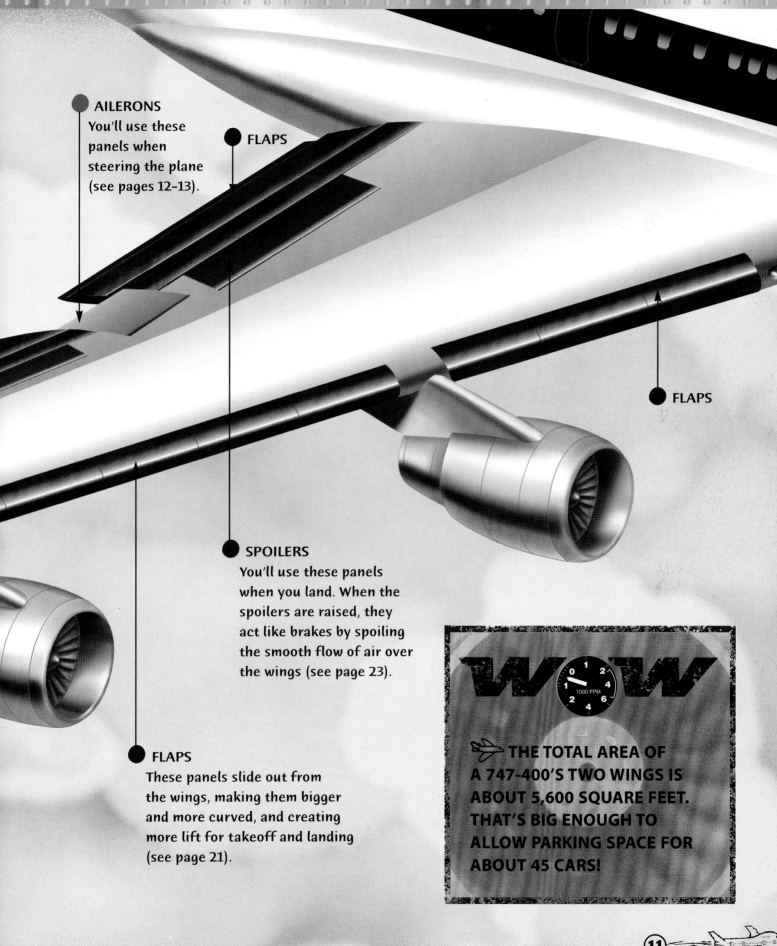

AILERONS
You'll use these panels when steering the plane (see pages 12–13).

FLAPS

FLAPS

SPOILERS
You'll use these panels when you land. When the spoilers are raised, they act like brakes by spoiling the smooth flow of air over the wings (see page 23).

FLAPS
These panels slide out from the wings, making them bigger and more curved, and creating more lift for takeoff and landing (see page 21).

WOW

1000 FPM

THE TOTAL AREA OF A 747-400'S TWO WINGS IS ABOUT 5,600 SQUARE FEET. THAT'S BIG ENOUGH TO ALLOW PARKING SPACE FOR ABOUT 45 CARS!

STEERING

Your plane is now about 33,000 feet above the ground—high enough for you to stop climbing. Gently push the control column forward until the plane is flying level. It's time to learn more about steering!

CONTROL SURFACES

You've already used the control column during take-off and now you need it to steer the plane. The column is connected to panels called ailerons on the wings and to elevators on the tail.

● ELEVATORS

AILERONS

CLIMBING AND DIVING

Steering a plane isn't just about turning to the left or right—it's also about climbing and diving. When you pull the control column toward you, the elevators tilt up. This pushes the plane's tail down and its nose up into a climb. When you push the control column away from you, the elevators tilt down. The tail points up and the plane's nose points down and you dip into a dive.

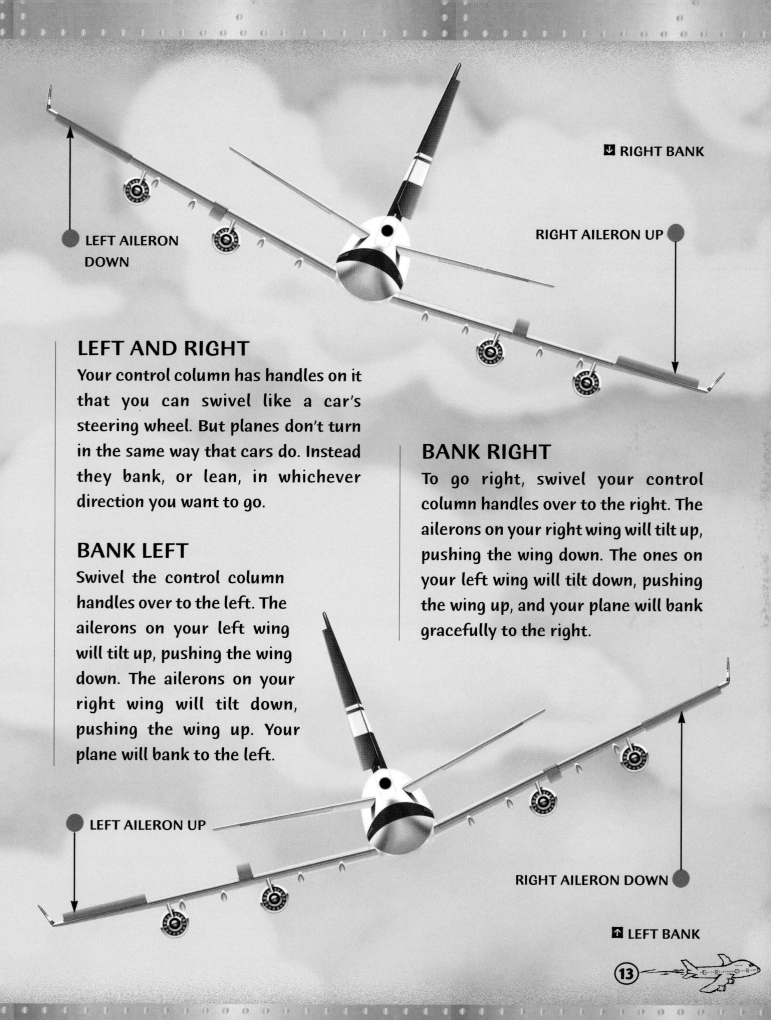

RIGHT BANK

LEFT AILERON DOWN

RIGHT AILERON UP

LEFT AND RIGHT

Your control column has handles on it that you can swivel like a car's steering wheel. But planes don't turn in the same way that cars do. Instead they bank, or lean, in whichever direction you want to go.

BANK LEFT

Swivel the control column handles over to the left. The ailerons on your left wing will tilt up, pushing the wing down. The ailerons on your right wing will tilt down, pushing the wing up. Your plane will bank to the left.

BANK RIGHT

To go right, swivel your control column handles over to the right. The ailerons on your right wing will tilt up, pushing the wing down. The ones on your left wing will tilt down, pushing the wing up, and your plane will bank gracefully to the right.

LEFT AILERON UP

RIGHT AILERON DOWN

LEFT BANK

NAVIGATION

You're cruising high above the clouds now, heading off across the world. How can you tell which way to go? There are no signposts or landmarks up here! Luckily for you, your plane's computers will show you the way.

FINDING YOUR WAY

Finding out where you are and in which direction you're traveling is called navigation. It's very important to be able to navigate accurately when you're flying long distances—getting lost would be disastrous!

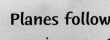
⬆ AN AERIAL in the plane's nose picks up radio-beacon signals.

TUNED IN

Planes follow set routes from airport to airport. Along these routes are beacons that beam out radio signals to show their position. Each beacon has its own signal that your plane can tune in to like a radio station.

RADIO
MAGNETIC NAVIGATION
INDICATOR DISPLAY

FLIGHT
MANAGEMENT
SYSTEM

the airport you've just left into the FMS and the one for the airport you're going to (your First Officer will tell you the codes). A needle on an instrument called the Radio Magnetic Indicator will then point in the direction of the first beacon on your route. Steer your plane in that direction to head for the beacon. When you get there, the needle will then point to your next beacon and so on until you reach the airport.

NAVIGATION INSTRUMENTS

The Navigation Display shows how far the plane has traveled on its route.

BEACON

Radio beacons are often hundreds of miles apart.

WAY TO GO

Your Flight Management System (FMS) will help you to navigate. The FMS is the computer system to your right that stores all of the set routes and beacons around the world.

Every airport in the world has its own code name. Type the code for

YOU CAN USE SATELLITES CIRCLING THE EARTH IN SPACE TO HELP YOU NAVIGATE! THE SATELLITES BEAM DOWN SIGNALS THAT THE PLANE'S COMPUTERS USE TO WORK OUT WHERE YOU ARE. THE INFORMATION IS SHOWN ON YOUR NAVIGATION DISPLAY.

COMPUTERS

Your computers do a lot more than help you to navigate. In fact, your 747 is such a complicated machine that you'd find it almost impossible to fly your plane without their help.

PRIMARY FLIGHT DISPLAY
(see page 17)

CENTER SCREENS
(see page 17)

NAVIGATION DISPLAY
(see page 15)

FLIGHT MANAGEMENT SYSTEM
(see page 15)

SCREEN SHOW

You and the First Officer each have your own sets of screens, apart from the center screens (3) which you share. The Primary Flight Display (1) and the Navigation Display (2) are the most important screens on the flight deck. You and your First Officer will need to watch these screens all through the flight. As the screens are directly in front of you, they're easy to keep an eye on.

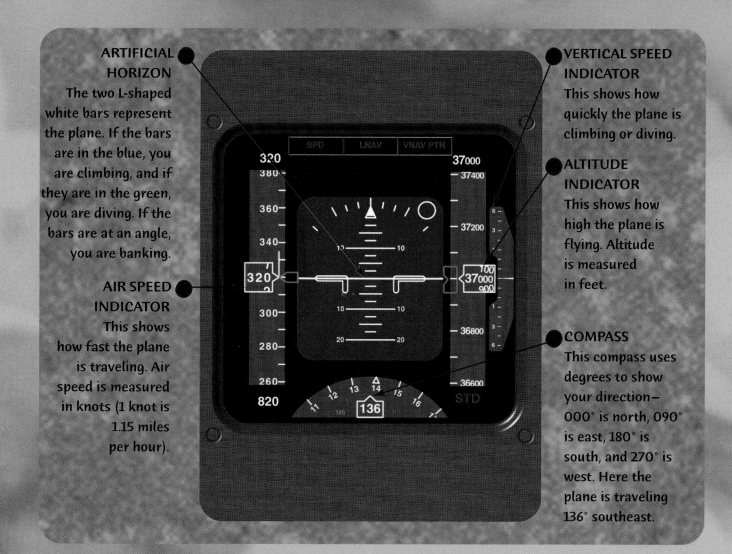

ARTIFICIAL HORIZON
The two L-shaped white bars represent the plane. If the bars are in the blue, you are climbing, and if they are in the green, you are diving. If the bars are at an angle, you are banking.

AIR SPEED INDICATOR
This shows how fast the plane is traveling. Air speed is measured in knots (1 knot is 1.15 miles per hour).

VERTICAL SPEED INDICATOR
This shows how quickly the plane is climbing or diving.

ALTITUDE INDICATOR
This shows how high the plane is flying. Altitude is measured in feet.

COMPASS
This compass uses degrees to show your direction— 000° is north, 090° is east, 180° is south, and 270° is west. Here the plane is traveling 136° southeast.

↑ PRIMARY FLIGHT DISPLAY

THE CENTER PAIRING

The two center screens (3) tell you how well the plane is working and warn you of any problems. The top screen shows information about the engines, such as temperature and speed. The bottom screen can tell you about fuel use and whether all the electrical equipment is working.

↑ THE LINES on the upper screen show that the engines are working properly.

STORMY WEATHER

You've been flying in perfect weather conditions high above the clouds for most of your journey. But now, as you begin to descend toward your destination airport, you spot a huge dark storm cloud straight ahead of you!

WEATHER FORECASTER

Turn on the weather radar switch (see page 5). When you do this, the radar dish in your plane's nose beams radio signals at the cloud.

⬆ THE RADIO SIGNALS bounce back off the cloud. These tell the plane's radar computer how big and how close the cloud really is.

The next thing to do is to check your Navigation Display (see page 19). A colored picture of the storm cloud has been flashed on it from the weather radar's computer.

BUMPY RIDE

The storm cloud is gigantic. It will take too long to fly around, so you're going to have to fly through it, steering around the worst of the weather.

↑ THE CLOUD'S STORMIEST AREAS appear as a bright red color on your Navigation Display—try to avoid those areas!

The rough conditions inside clouds are called turbulence. Going through strong turbulence feels like a roller coaster ride. You need to warn the passengers and crew.

At the end of the control panel to your right is a handset that lets you talk to the whole plane. Ask everyone to fasten their seat belts—it's going to be a bumpy ride! But tell them not to worry as you'll be through the storm fairly quickly.

COMING IN TO LAND

You're out of the storm cloud now, so let the passengers and crew know. As you continue your descent, your headset radio crackles—an Air Traffic Controller at your destination airport is on the line.

DESCENT

Air Traffic Control has called to ask you to drop to 900 feet to begin your approach to the runway. Push the control column forward until the altitude indicator on your Primary Flight Display (see page 17) shows you're flying at the right height. Then pull back on the column to level out your plane and continue your approach to the runway.

⬆ AIR TRAFFIC CONTROL uses huge radar screens to watch every plane in the area.

COMING IN TO LAND

When you're about 5 miles from the airport, your plane picks up two radio signals from the runway. These signals will guide you in to land. One of them gives you the correct angle of descent toward the runway. The other helps you to keep in line with the center of the runway.

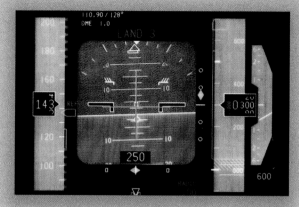

⬆ THE PINK CROSS on your Primary Flight Display marks the correct path.

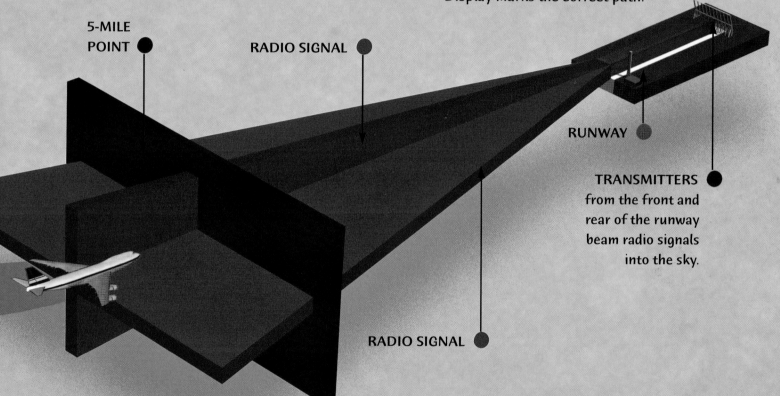

5-MILE POINT

RADIO SIGNAL

RUNWAY

TRANSMITTERS from the front and rear of the runway beam radio signals into the sky.

RADIO SIGNAL

ARTIFICIAL AID

The airport's landing beams will make a pink cross appear on the artificial horizon of the Primary Flight Display. Use your control column to keep the white bars lined up with the cross, and the plane will fly on the right course.

SLOW DOWN

Cut your speed now, or you'll be going too fast to stop on the runway. But slowing down means you'll lose lift and descend too quickly. So pull the wing flaps lever down (see page 5) to make the flaps slide out from the wing edges and create more lift.

TOUCHDOWN

You're just about 200 feet above the ground now and the runway is rushing toward you. Your First Officer pulls the lever on his left (see page 5) that lowers the plane's wheels—are you ready to land?

TOUCHDOWN

The wheels are down and the First Officer says,

"Decide."

If the runway's clear and it's safe to land you say,

"Land."

At 30 feet, gently pull the control column back, and the plane's nose tips up. This is called flaring and it helps you to stop losing lift too quickly. Pull back the engine levers (see page 8) to cut the engine power, and the plane touches down on the runway.

STOP

As you touch down, the spoilers (see pages 10–11) automatically spring up from the wings. Air presses against the spoilers and starts to slow the plane down. Now say,

"Reverse."

The First Officer puts the engines into reverse, and small flaps, called vents, open up in the sides of the engines. Instead of the thrust coming out of the back of the engine it now shoots forward out of the vents. This helps to slow the plane's forward movement. At the same time the wheel brakes automatically come on, and you roll gently to a halt.

CONGRATULATIONS

You've just completed your first flight! In less than an hour the plane will be refueled, cleaned, and ready to fly back home. Another crew will take the controls for that flight—it's time you took a well-deserved break!

WELL DONE, CAPTAIN!

⬇ YOUR PLANE will be traveling at about 175 miles per hour when it first touches down on the runway.

INDEX

Photographs on pages 4, 5, 7, 8, 15, 16, 17, 19, 21, cover and poster used with the permission of The Boeing Company.

Photographs on pages 2-3 and 20 courtesy of Tony Stone and the Aviation Picture Library.

Illustrations by Roger Goode and Robert Holder at Beehive Illustration.

Edited by Paul Harrison.
Designed by Louise Jackson.

Text copyright © 2000 by Ian Graham
Illustrations copyright © 2000 by Walker Books Ltd.

First U.S. edition 2000

Library of Congress Cataloging-in-Publication Data is available.

Library of Congress Catalog Card Number 99-059193

ISBN 0-7636-1278-2

10 9 8 7 6 5 4 3 2 1

Printed in Hong Kong

This book was typeset in Humana and TF Avion. The illustrations were done using Photoshop and Illustrator.

Candlewick Press
2067 Massachusetts Avenue
Cambridge, Massachusetts 02140